TRACKS IN THE WILD

BETSY BOWEN

Little, Brown and Company
Boston Toronto London

Dedicated to Eric, Jeremy, and Philip,
who are making their paths in life
and leaving signs and footprints of their own

Acknowledgments to Chel Anderson, Rick Anderson, Eric Beckert, Billy Blackwell, Jim Bowen, Tom Brown, Jr., Chris Cole, Carol DeSain, Tom Fagan, Andrew and Genevieve Gorny, Joyce Klees, P. S. Lovejoy, Olaus Murie, Betty Lovejoy Olsen, Mike Schelmeske, and Fritz Sobanja, all for showing me something of the wonder of life in the woods; and special thanks to Stan Malless

First Edition

Library of Congress Cataloging-in-Publication Data

Bowen, Betsy.
Tracks in the wild / Betsy Bowen. — 1st ed.
p. cm.
Summary: Explores the habits and behavior of thirteen northwoods animals by discussing the various tracks and signs left by them.
ISBN 0-316-10377-2
1. Animal tracks — Juvenile literature. [1. Animals — Habits and behavior. 2. Animal tracks.] I. Title.
QL768.B69 1993
596 — dc20 92-28691

10 9 8 7 6 5 4 3 2 1

BER

Published simultaneously in Canada
by Little, Brown & Company (Canada) Limited

Printed in the United States of America

The pictures in this book are woodblock prints, made by carving the design and the big letters, backwards, into a flat block of white pine, rolling black ink onto the block, and then printing on a Vandercook No. 4 letterpress housed at the Historic Grand Marais Art Colony. The colors are then painted on each print.

Man did not weave the web of life.
He is only a strand in it.

— Chief Seattle

No two robins are ever the same . . . each is as different as you and I, and we can never exhaust the possibilities of learning something new each time we observe a robin. This is also true of everything else in life, every experience, every situation, every bird, tree, rock, water, and leaf, for we can never know enough about anything. Finally, you do not even begin to know an animal until you touch it, and feel its spirit. Then and only then can you ever begin to know.

— Stalking Wolf, Apache tracker

Bears, wolves, moose, otters, and many other wild animals live around me here in the northwoods of Minnesota, but I don't often see them. I know they are near only by the tracks they leave.

Each track tells a story. As you follow the marks an animal has left behind, you get to know it: where it goes, what it likes to eat, when it runs, and why. As you begin to see the patterns in the tracks, you will begin to see the variations. Each set of tracks is unique, because each animal's life is different from every other's and each day its path is a little different from the one it took the day before.

A track is more than just a footprint. Grass might be bent over, tooth marks might be left on a branch, or a stone might be turned upside down. Hair might be sticking to a bush where it scraped off as the animal walked by. There might be a noticeable smell. A web is a sign of the spider's weaving but may also show a disturbance from an insect or animal that bumped into it as it passed by.

This book will tell you about the wild animals whose tracks I see in the woods here. Their footprints are shown life size. When you look for these tracks on your own, remember that at the end of each track is the animal who left behind these signs of its passing. And whether or not you reach the animal, you will have begun to know it by following in its path.

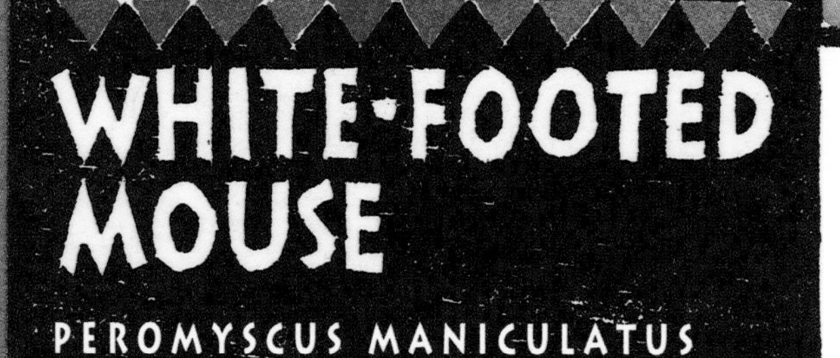

WHITE-FOOTED MOUSE

PEROMYSCUS MANICULATUS

One should pay attention to even the smallest crawling creature for these too may have a valuable lesson to teach us, and even the smallest ant may wish to communicate to a man.
— Black Elk, Oglala Sioux

The tiny white-footed mouse, also called the deer mouse, is no bigger than my thumb. It leaves delicate tracks, which often begin at one tree and end at the next. It is a great climber and often makes nests in hollow trunks or branches of trees. Sometimes I hear deer mice as I am falling asleep, when they are just beginning their nightly activities. They seem to be talking to me, in their soft, squeaky, singing voices, saying, "This is our life. We go out into the darkness now to explore, staying out of the way of the fox and the coyote and the great horned owl, so that we can come back to the nest with food to keep us alive for the long winter." All night they scurry about, gathering and storing lots of seeds in tree hollows, in burrows under roots, and in spaces between rocks.

ERMINE

MUSTELA ERMINEA

An ermine makes twin footprints, side by side, in a narrow zigzag path in the snow as it bounds along with front feet and hind feet together. It makes energetic leaps, jumping this way and that, hunting for mice, chipmunks, and birds at night, and it may even make a den in the home of a mouse after eating it! If you squeak like a mouse, a curious ermine may come out to have a look at you.

The white ermine of winter becomes a brown, short-tailed weasel in the summer. It gives off a skunklike odor, which you may notice near its den. You can learn to be a good tracker from ermines by being like them: alert — always looking, always listening.

RUFFED GROUSE

BONASA UMBELLUS

Grouse are more adapted to living on the ground than in the air. Their tracks are those of walking birds, who make a narrow pattern by placing one foot in front of the other in a line. (Tracks of birds who fly more than they walk will show side-by-side prints, since they hop when they are on the ground.) As grouse walk, their heads bob back and forth in a comical rhythm. They fly for short distances and often roost in trees.

A mother grouse and her chicks once wandered out of the woods and into my yard as I was sitting and reading. I was thrilled. I tried not to blink as I watched them poke around in the grass, searching for insects and seeds. The mother clucked quietly to keep the chicks from going too far away.

In winter, a line of grouse tracks may lead to a spruce tree, where bare spots on the branches show that needles have been nibbled off. To stay warm, grouse bury themselves in snow. They stand in one spot and dig with their feet until they have sunk far enough. As you walk past, the snow may explode in a flurry with a flustered grouse, who has heard the vibrations of your footsteps through the earth.

PINE MARTEN

MARTES AMERICANA

"Tracks," said Piglet. "Paw-marks." He gave a little squeak of excitement. "Oh Pooh, do you think it's a-a-a woozle?"
— A. A. Milne, *Winnie-the-Pooh*

The marten is as elusive a creature as the woozle, and one winter evening, I was as excited as Piglet to see pine marten tracks near the cabin I was staying in. That night, the marten climbed up the cabin's unfinished log wall and once inside, started churning up the garbage, then raced frantically from one wall to the other when we shone a light on it. It was a beautiful animal, with its light-colored face, bright eyes, and long furry tail.

Members of the weasel family — which also includes ermines, minks, fishers, wolverines, and otters — martens are quick, wary creatures who can be seen most often at night. They are very agile and climb trees in pursuit of red squirrels for supper. They can travel many miles in a night, hunting for small mammals and birds, blueberries, pine nuts, and mountain ash berries. Their tracks show five toes, whereas members of the dog family, which includes foxes, wolves, and coyotes, have four-toed prints.

SNOWSHOE HARE

LEPUS AMERICANUS

What is life?
It is the flash of a buffalo in the night.
It is the breath of a butterfly in the wintertime.
It is the little shadow which runs across the grass and loses itself in the sunset.
— Crowfoot, Orator of the Blackfoot Confederacy

The movements of the snowshoe hare are fleeting: swift and gentle like a shadow or a breath of air. The shy and humble hares are always on the move and don't make any permanent homes, just hidden resting places out of sight of the foxes, wolves, and owls who might eat them. The babies are born with fur and their eyes already open. Within a few hours, they are able to run.

Snowshoe hares usually spend their days asleep under evergreens or brush piles, but at night they search for food. They eat only plants. You might see ends of low-growing pine branches nipped off, or parts of spruce branches with the needles eaten.

In summer the snowshoe hare is brown, and in winter its fur turns white, to help the hare avoid being seen by predators. Its hind feet are much longer than the front, with spread-out toes that work like snowshoes to keep the hare running lightly on top of the snow. Its tracks are common here in winter, the two big hind footprints surrounding the small front ones at each jump.

RED FOX

VULPES FULVA

The red fox is direct and observant. In folktales, the fox is often the one who demonstrates swiftness and cunning, or the one who, by strength and courage, gains special knowledge and helps people. The fox walks by placing its feet in a straight line. As the front foot comes up off the ground, the smaller hind foot is placed in exactly the same spot, leaving a dainty trail. You can practice fox-walking by putting one foot directly ahead of the other. This is a good way to walk in the woods and will help you to think like a fox while you hunt for animals to watch.

Foxes live in dens underground or in hollows in rocks, especially when the six or so pups are born in the spring. But they also may sleep curled up in the open and have even been snowed over in a storm. A parent fox will drag and hide a field mouse under leaves so the pups must find it. This way they will learn to hunt. Foxes also eat strawberries and swim in the summer, just as you might like to do.

COMMON RAVEN

CORVUS CORAX

The most important of all the creatures are the wingeds, for they are nearest to the heavens, and are not bound to the earth, as are the four-legged, or little crawling people. . . . They see everything that happens on the earth.
— Black Elk, Oglala Sioux

The Sioux respect the raven for its watchfulness, and the raven is also important in Eskimo legend as the creator of the earth. Ravens are large and powerful-looking birds. I often see them here, flying alone or in pairs across the sky, soaring and tumbling in the air. They can flip upside down as they chase and evade and sky-dance with each other. Ravens do not kill for food but rather eat animals that have already died. They apparently have a way of calling other ravens as well as wolves when one has found good feeding. Their tracks will most often show up around a feeding area.

Ravens have been found to have a complex social structure, sometimes gathering in colonies, where they roost together in tall trees, sharing food, and even mourning together when one of them dies.

Let a man decide upon his favorite animal and make a study of it — let him learn to understand its sounds and motions. The animals want to communicate with man, but Wakan-Tanka [The Spirit of All Things] does not intend that they shall do so directly — man must do the greater part in securing an understanding.

— Brave Buffalo, Oglala Sioux

My favorite animal is the considerate and playful otter. Several times, river otters have looked up at me from the water: it always felt special and made me wish to communicate with them. I sense they would tell me to play often and happily with my friends and family and to take good care of them. Otters are never far from water, making their dens in the banks of rivers or lakes. They eat fish, frogs, and crayfish. The adventuresome creatures may travel for miles from their dens, except when the three to four young are born in the spring. Both parents care for the young, and they stay together as a family longer than most animals. They have a broad vocabulary of chuckles, screeches, and hisses.

Tracks of the otters' webbed feet will often show near the sliding chutes that these exuberant creatures make in wet mud or snow to play follow-the-leader.

BEAVER

CASTOR CANADENSIS

What is man without the beasts?
If all the beasts were gone, men would die from a great loneliness of the spirit.
For whatever happens to the beasts soon happens to man.
— Chief Seattle

Beavers are the largest of all the North American rodents. The webs that make a beaver's hind feet good for swimming will show in its footprints in mud along the bank of a pond, unless its wide, flat tail has dragged across the track. Beavers spend summer days gnawing aspen, birch, and willow trees with their strong front teeth. They eat the bark and use the logs for building dams and lodges. These ingenious animals create their living environment by changing the landscape: they build dams to create ponds with water deep enough for them both to swim and to build their lodges. In late spring or summer, three or four babies are born in each lodge, and within a week they can swim.

To supply fur to make fancy top hats for rich European men, much beaver trapping was done here in the 1600s and 1700s, and by 1800, beavers were nearly extinct. Now there are more beavers because trapping is regulated.

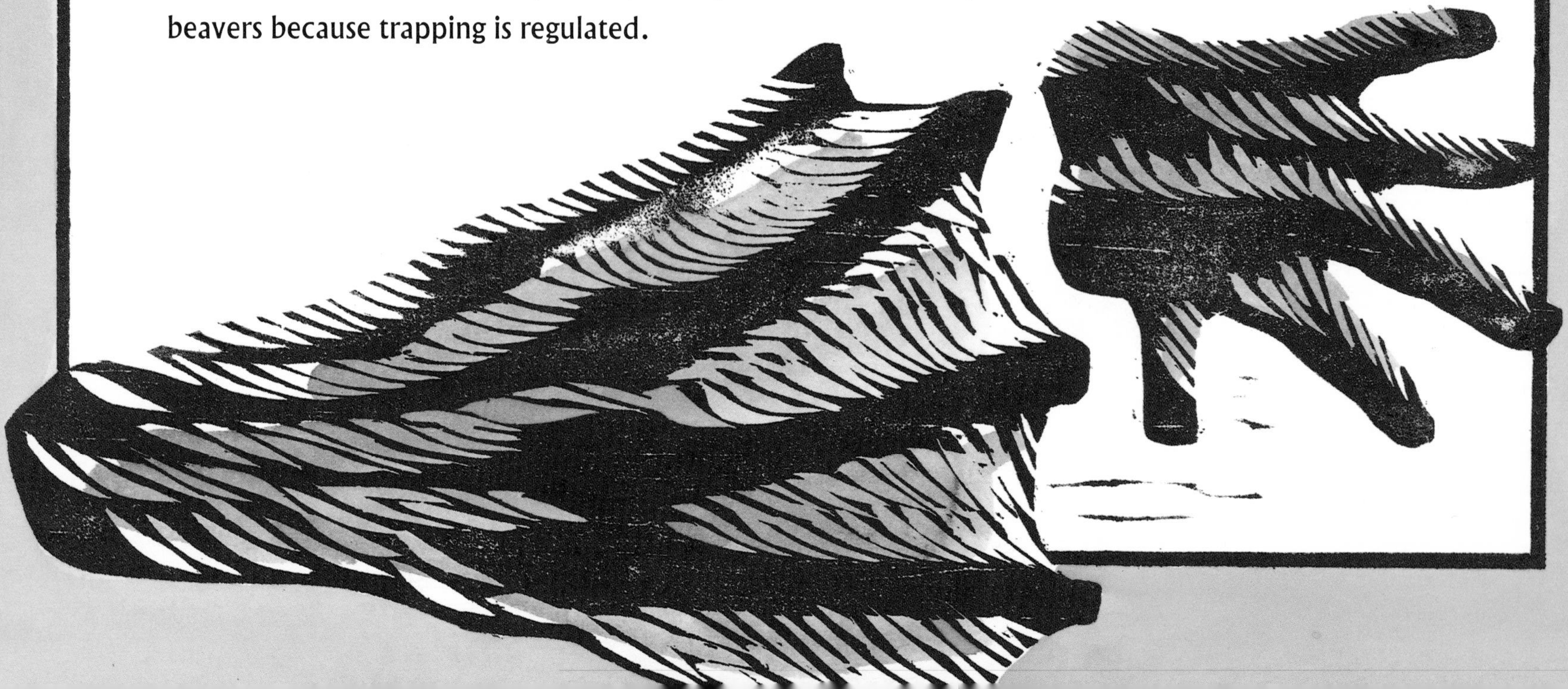

GRAY WOLF

CANIS LUPUS

You ought to follow the example of shunk-tokecha *[gray wolf]. Even when he is surprised and runs for his life, he will pause to take one more look at you before he enters his final retreat. So you must take a second look at everything you see.*

— Old uncle of Ohiyesa (Charles Eastman)

By their custom of stopping at a good viewpoint and taking in all they can see, wolves teach us to be careful observers. They are great wanderers. With their territory ranging up to one hundred square miles, they see much and know much. They travel together in extended families, cooperating to find food and to watch out for each other. They eat deer, moose, and small animals and birds. Ravens often travel near wolves and share their food.

Tracks of a gray wolf (also called a timber wolf) look much like big dog tracks, with four toes on each foot and with the toenails showing in a clear print.

Wolves are not aggressive toward people; they keep their distance. The times I have awakened in the night to hear their group howling songs, I could not stop listening.

WHITE-TAILED DEER

ODOCOILEUS VIRGINIANUS

Deer always seem to be munching leaves, twigs, and bark. As they move around their regular feeding paths, they will eat ten to twelve pounds a day. Along the edge of a lake here where deer have eaten regularly, all the lower branches of the trees will be gone up to the height of the deer's reach. Deer are graceful and alert. They are seen often in the northwoods, leaping higher than seems possible, their white tails up when they are startled.

When the snow begins to get deep, the deer move down out of the hills to spend the winter toward Lake Superior, where there is less snow. The feet of a deer are hoofed, and small for the size of the animal, so they sink far into the snow. The track appears at the bottom of a narrow hole. In spring the tracks will often show in the soft mud along the side of a gravel road. There I have sometimes seen tiny hoofprints of a fawn, and am always touched. They're so like the mother's tracks, yet even more fragile and delicate.

MOOSE

ALCES ALCES

Moose tracks are big, an unmistakable record of the wanderings of this clumsy and majestic animal. Because of their long legs — longer than a kindergartner is tall — their footprints are far apart. I have sometimes seen moose tracks underwater in ponds and lakes, when the sun was shining through the shallow water, lighting up the bottom. Moose come to the water each morning and evening to feed on the aquatic plants. They wade right in, dunk their huge heads under for a bite, and come up with a splash, chewing the dripping weeds.

Moose were important animals to the Anishnabe people, Native Americans who lived near Lake Superior long ago and used the animals for food and clothing. They had much respect for the moose and drew them in pictographs, paintings on rock cliffs. Today Ojibwa women still make beautiful moccasins and mittens from moose hide. They decorate these items with beaded flower designs to celebrate woodland life.

BLACK BEAR

URSUS AMERICANUS

The bear has a soul like ours and his soul talks to mine and tells me what to do.

— Bear-with-White-Paws, Oglala Sioux

The bear is honored by Native Americans for its strength and its wisdom about healing, especially with herbs. Native peoples gained bear powers from dreams and visions and by observing what the bear does and what it eats. Bears dig up and eat many plants and roots. Their feet have five toes with strong claws, which are especially good for digging in the earth. Bears sleep during the winter, so their tracks are seldom seen in the snow; most often they will show up in the soft mud of early spring, when the bear wakes up hungry for grubs, berries, fish, and herbs.

Seeing the track of a bear is more startling to me than actually seeing a bear, perhaps because the track is close enough to touch. When I put my hand within the footprint, I feel the hugeness of the bear's furry presence and almost hear the rhythm of its breathing as I imagine it walking along and placing its foot in that spot.

But now ask the beasts, and let them teach you;
and the birds of the heavens, and let them tell you.
Or speak to the earth, and let it teach you.
— Job 12:7–8

From the mouse I have learned to be watchful, from the hare to be gentle, from the fox to be deliberate, from the otter to love life. A sense of animals' presence on the earth is important to me as a part of feeling connected to all things. Thank you, my animal teachers. I sing you honor and respect.

I hope animals will be teachers in your life, too. Watch for them often, and listen to what they have to say.